T
Black Rabbit

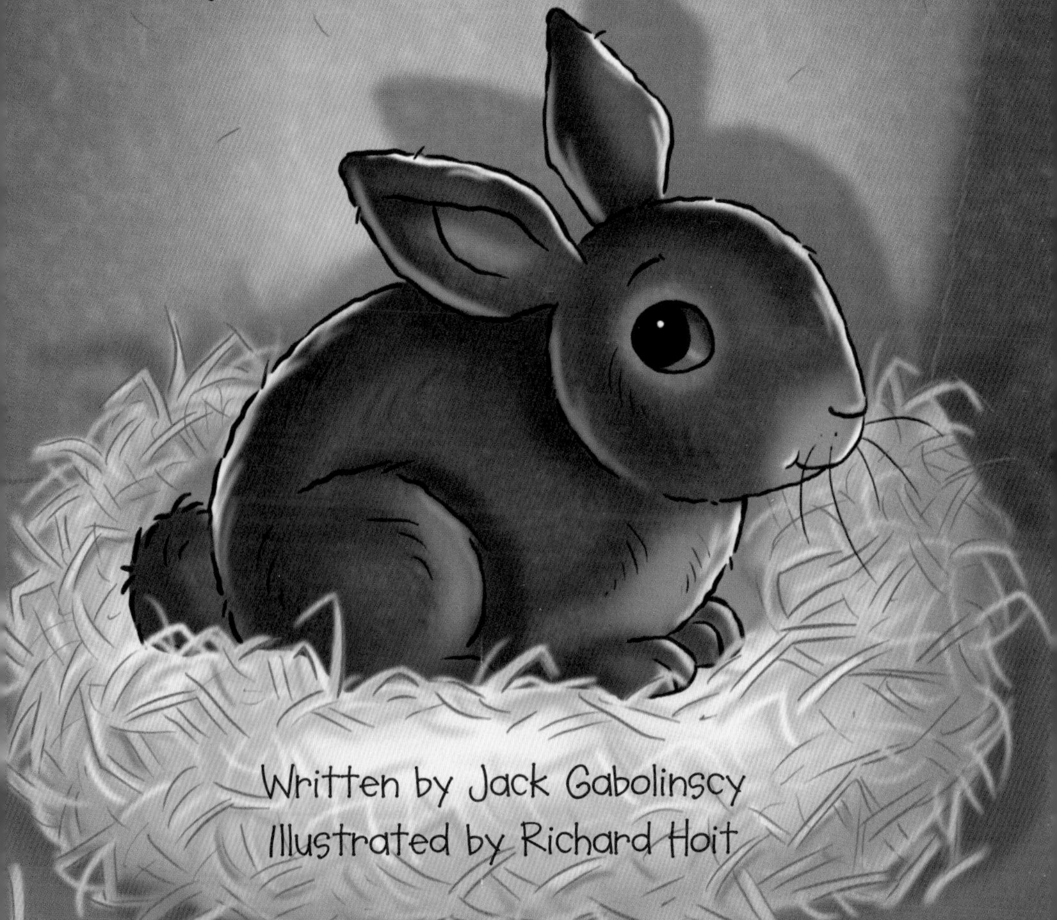

Written by Jack Gabolinscy
Illustrated by Richard Hoit

Harcourt Achieve
Rigby • Saxon • Steck-Vaughn

www.HarcourtAchieve.com
1.800.531.5015

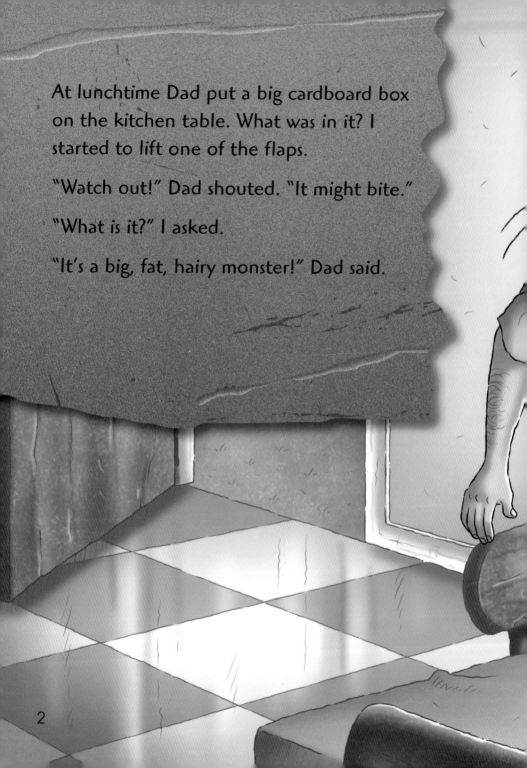

At lunchtime Dad put a big cardboard box on the kitchen table. What was in it? I started to lift one of the flaps.

"Watch out!" Dad shouted. "It might bite."

"What is it?" I asked.

"It's a big, fat, hairy monster!" Dad said.

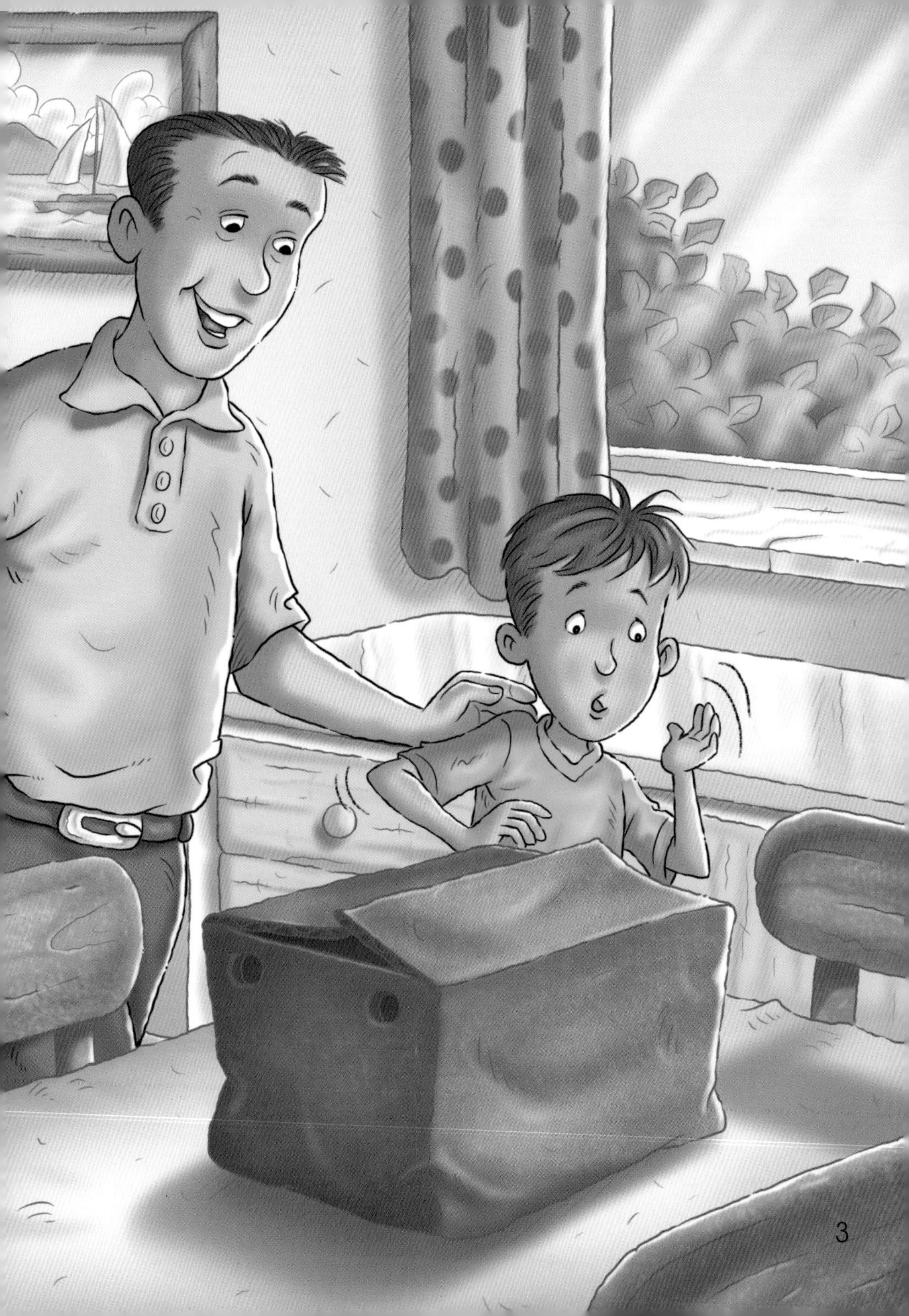

Dad opened the flaps on the box.
"I found it down in the pasture," he said.

Mom and Edward stretched their necks
to see inside.

"What is it?" I asked. "Will it really bite?"

"Ooooh!" said Mom. "It's so sweet."

"It's black," said Edward. "I've never
seen a wild black one before."

I jumped up and down trying to look
into the box. "What is it? Let me see!"

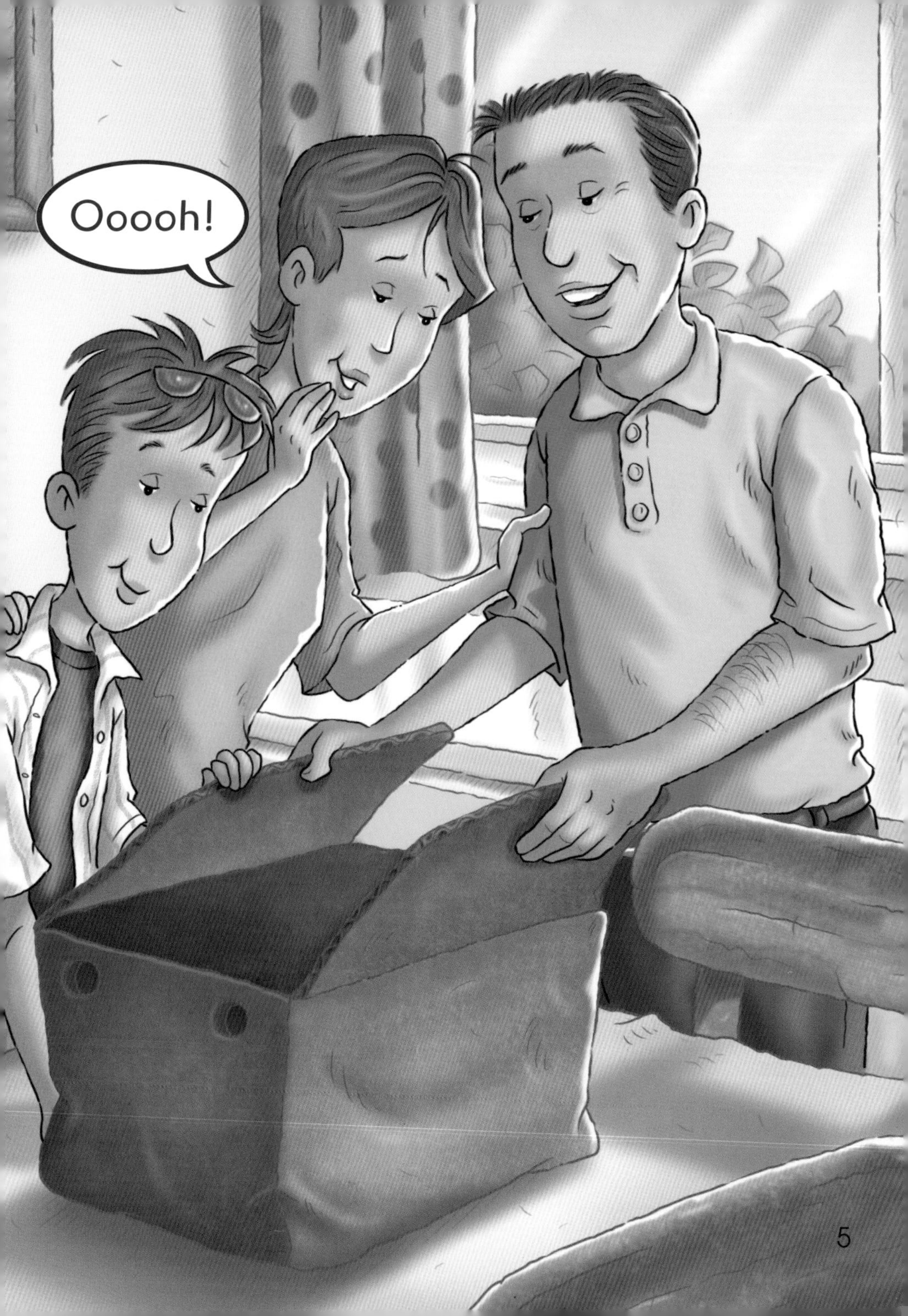
Ooooh!

Dad moved the box off the table and put it onto a chair. I looked in.

There in the box was a beautiful, black baby rabbit. It was huddled into a corner. Its ears were flat, and it was shivering with fear.

I closed the top again to stop it from being scared.

"Put it in your bedroom until it's not so frightened," said Mom.

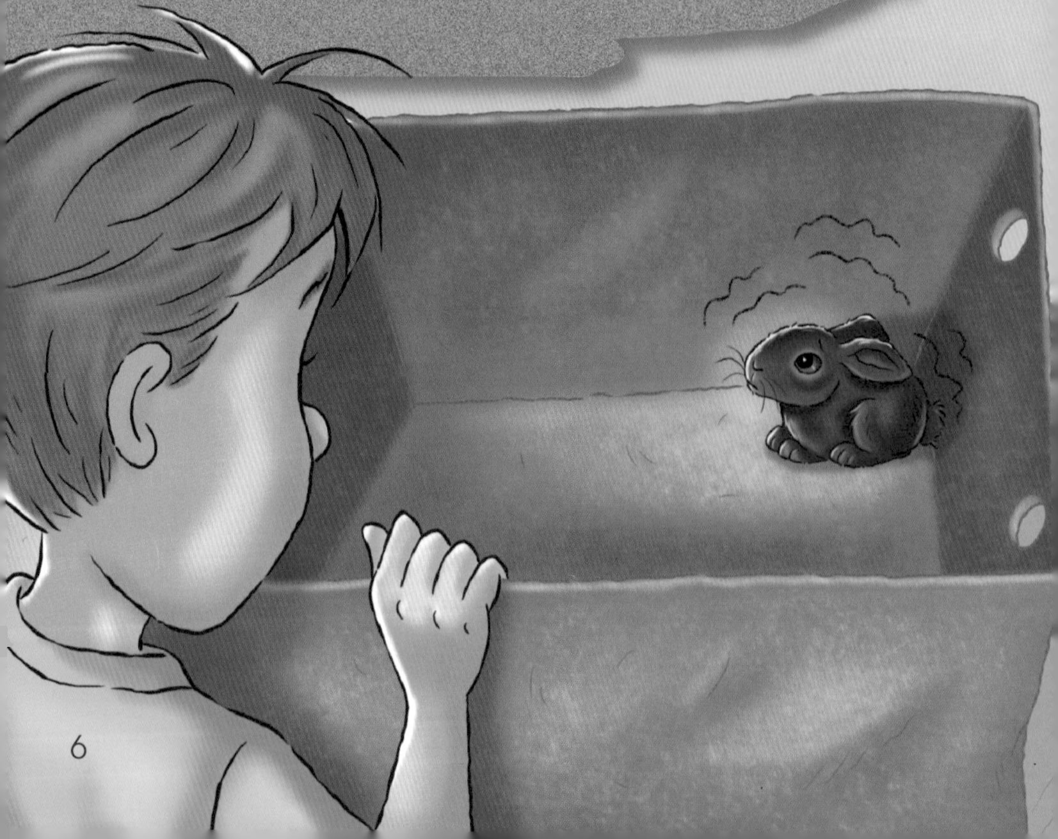

When everyone had gone, I opened
the box quietly and picked up the
rabbit. I talked to it softly so that it
would know I wasn't going to hurt it.
It snuggled into my arms.

It had big, round black eyes. Its nose
wriggled, and its ears lifted a bit.

Mom heated a baby bottle full of milk. It must have been hungry, because it drank half the bottle without stopping.

I got some straw for the box, and put the little rabbit in gently. Then I moved it next to the furnace. A few minutes later, it was sound asleep.

"I'll call you 'Midnight'," I whispered.

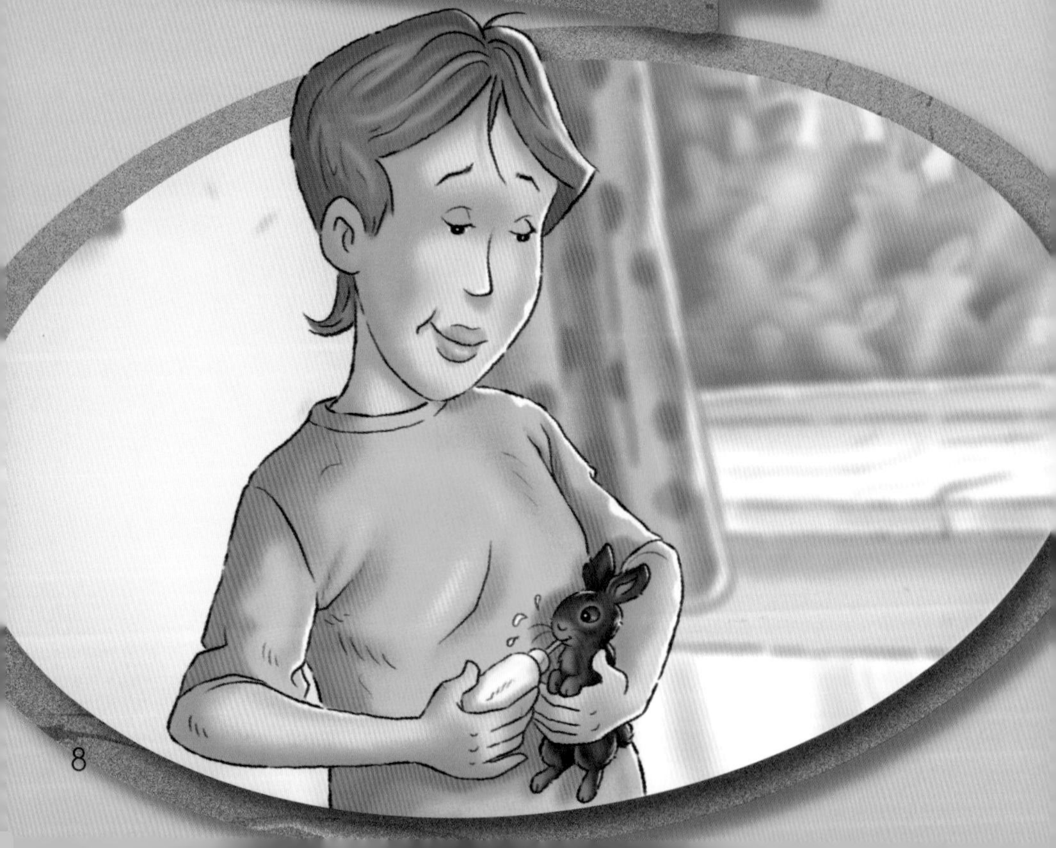

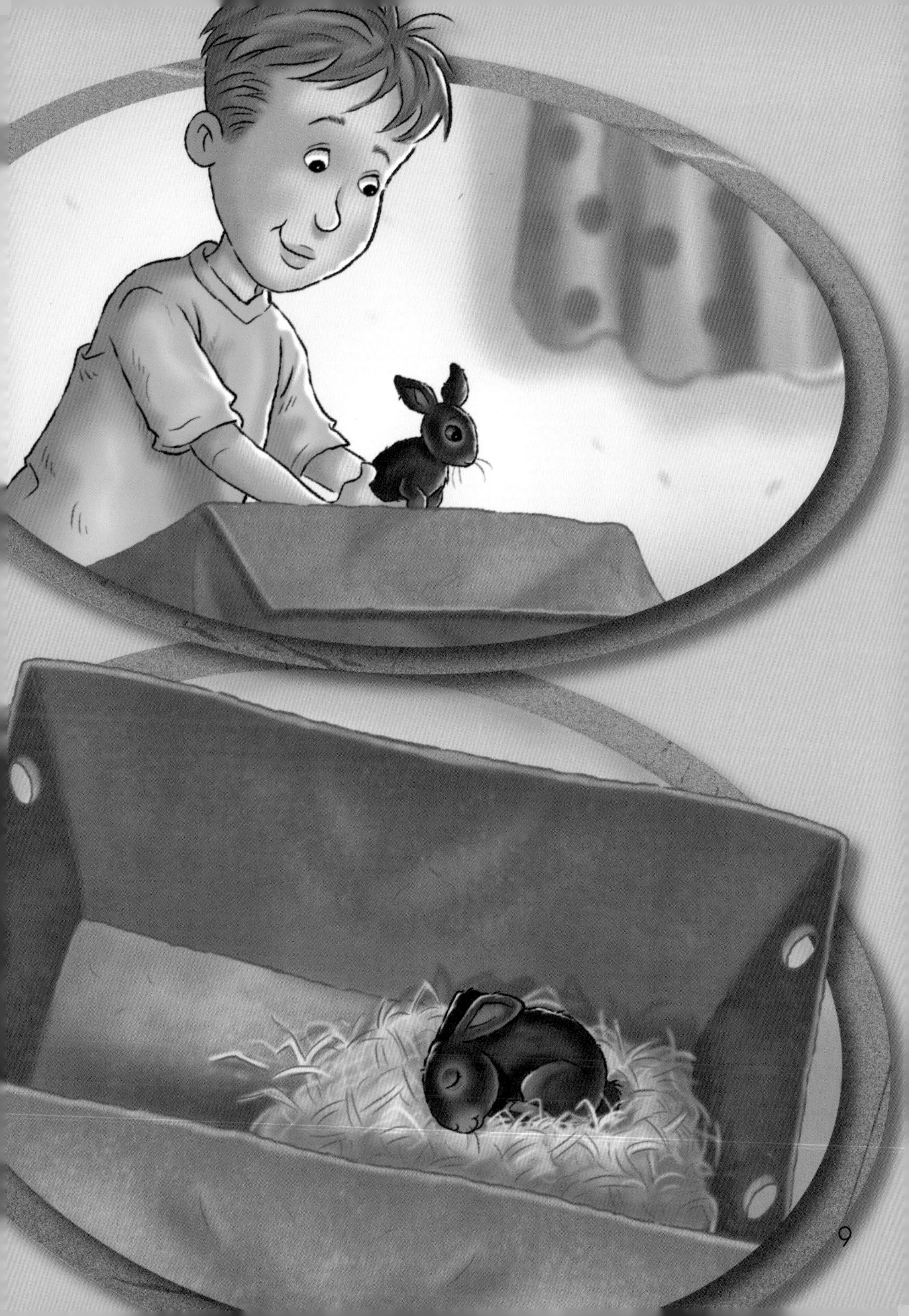

By lunchtime the next day, Midnight had stopped shaking. He was quite happy in his new home.

I felt a special pride in Midnight because I was the one who had made friends with him first and fed him.

We had a picnic lunch on the lawn. I couldn't wait to show Midnight off. I wanted everyone to see that I was his favorite person and that he was really my pet.

I put Midnight on my chest. I walked around with my hands under him, just in case he fell.

"Look!" I said. "He can hold on by himself." I took my hands away.

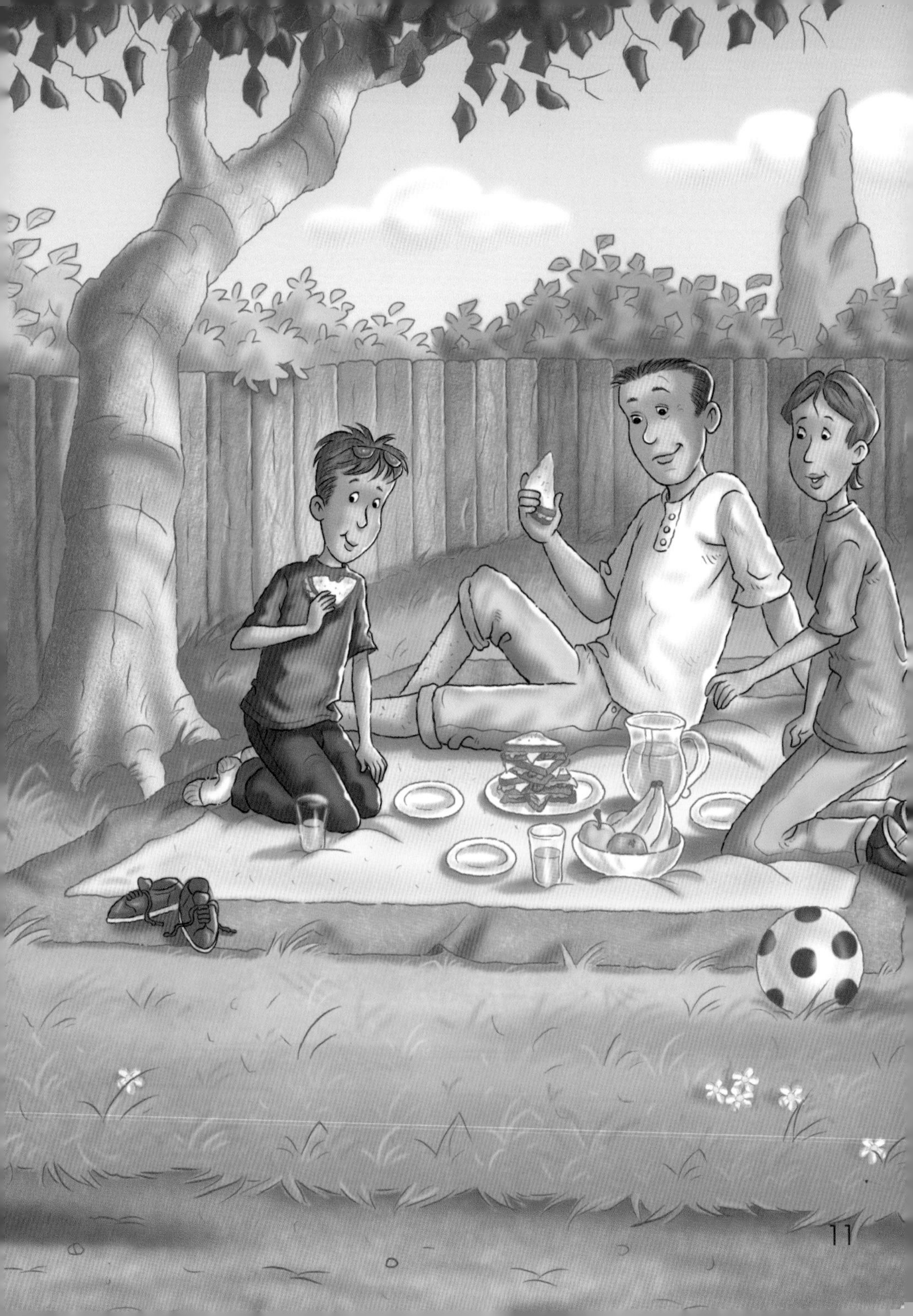

"Be careful," warned Mom. "He might fall."

"No, he won't," I said. "He holds on by himself."

Just then Midnight did fall. I made a wild grab to catch him. Instead of catching him, I knocked him further up into the air. Up he went, and down he fell. Crash! Right onto his head. Right on the concrete sidewalk.

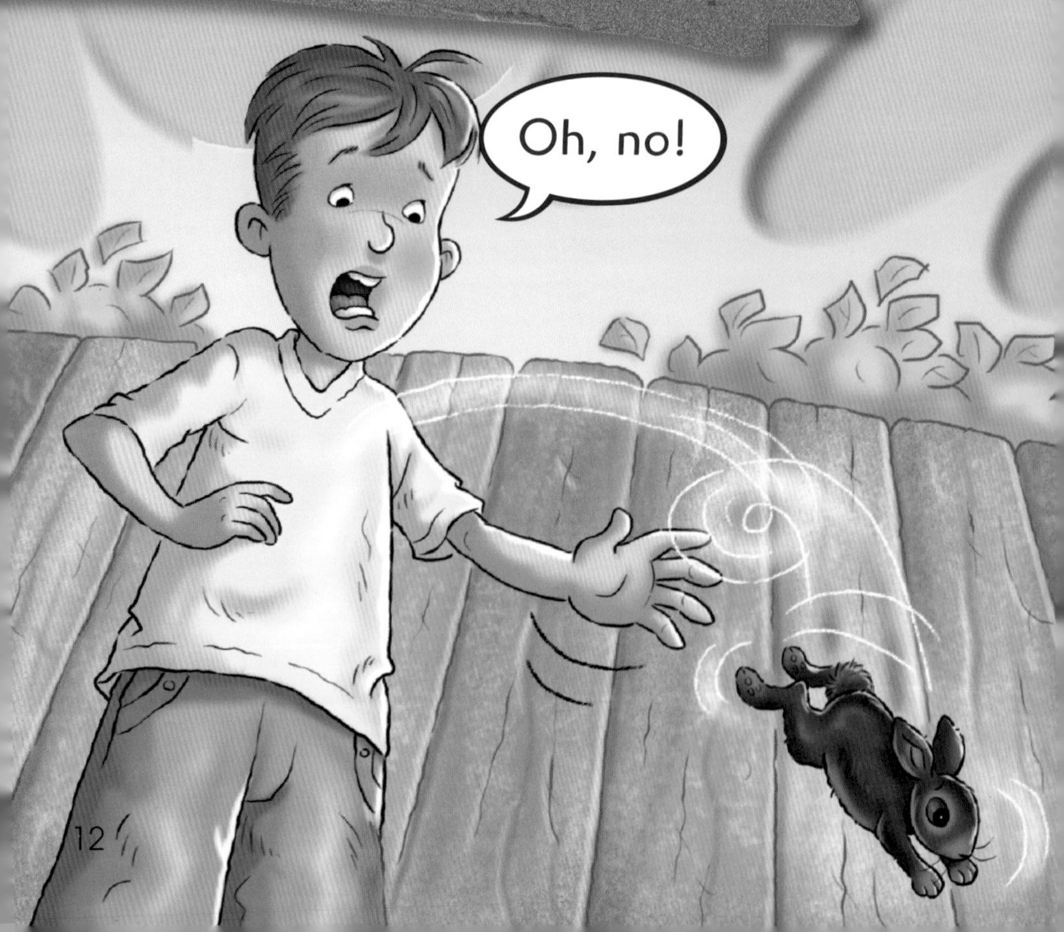
Oh, no!

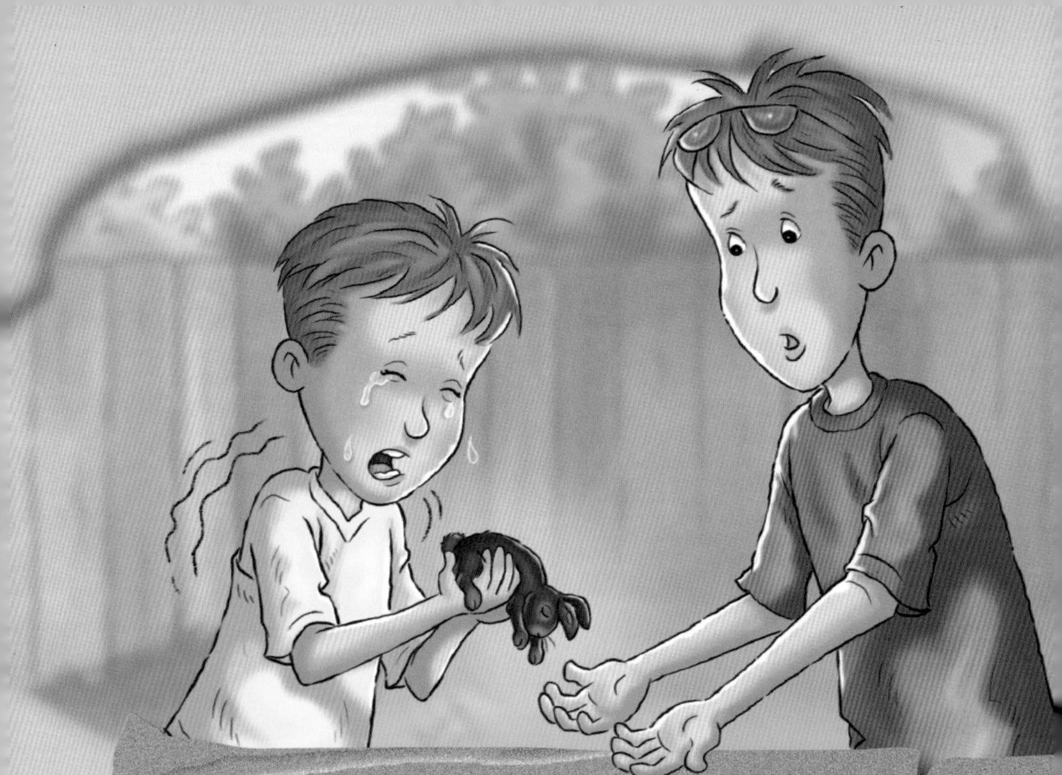

Nobody moved. Nobody said anything. Midnight lay still. I stood still. I couldn't believe what I had done.

I bent and picked up Midnight. He was like a soft rag doll. His legs and head hung down loosely. The tears squeezed from my eyes and ran down my cheeks.

Edward took Midnight from my hands. "I think he's broken his neck," he said. He put him back into his box gently.

It wasn't a very good picnic after that. Nobody said anything, and I felt so bad for killing Midnight. I was going to miss him. We hadn't had him long, but he'd become my best friend.

After lunch, Dad said, "I'll take Midnight with me and bury him down near the back of the farm."

I sat on the steps while Dad went to pick up Midnight's box. He looked into the box. Then he called to me. "You'd better have one last look, before I take him away," he said.

"I don't want to!" I cried.

"I think you should," said Dad.

I got to the box. I didn't want to look. I didn't want to see what I had done to poor Midnight.

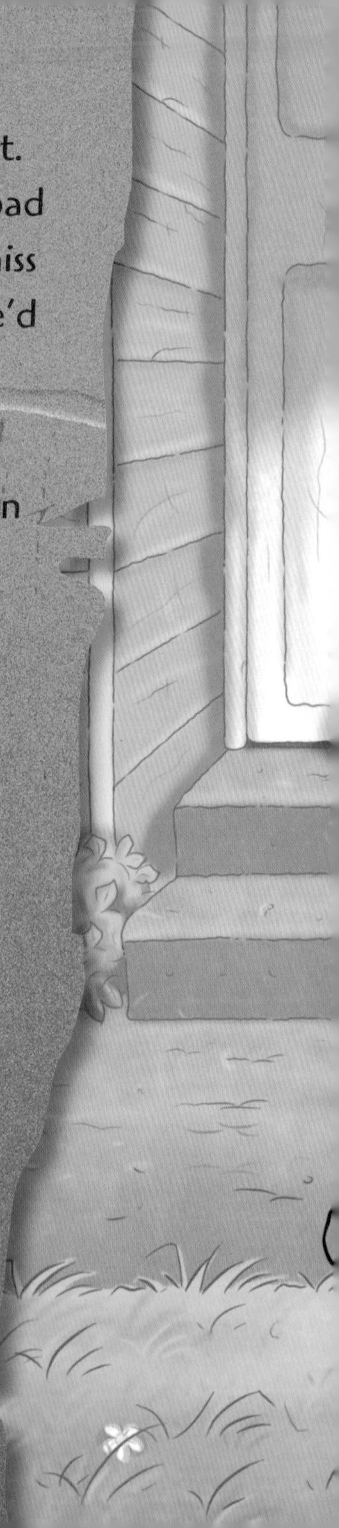

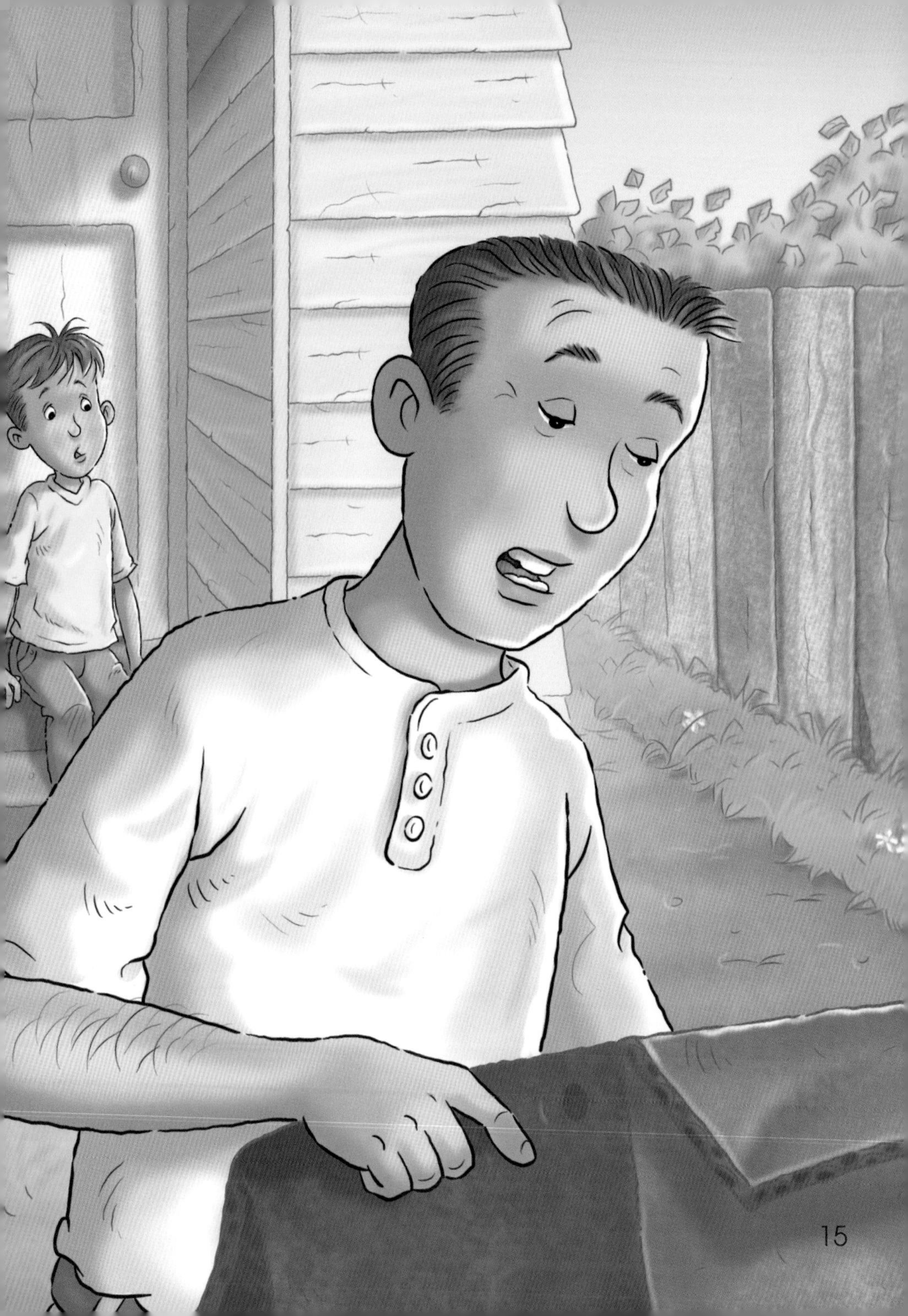

"Look!" said Dad.

I opened my eyes. There, on the bottom of the box was Midnight. His nose was wriggling, his eyes were shining, and his ears were up. He wasn't dead at all!

"He must have just been knocked out," said Edward. He picked Midnight up from the box and handed him to me. "Here," he said kindly. "You have to remember to hold him with two hands."

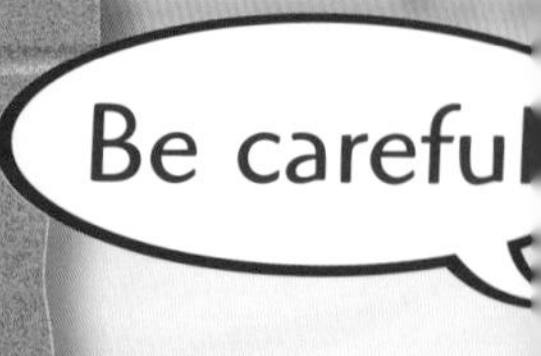
Be carefu

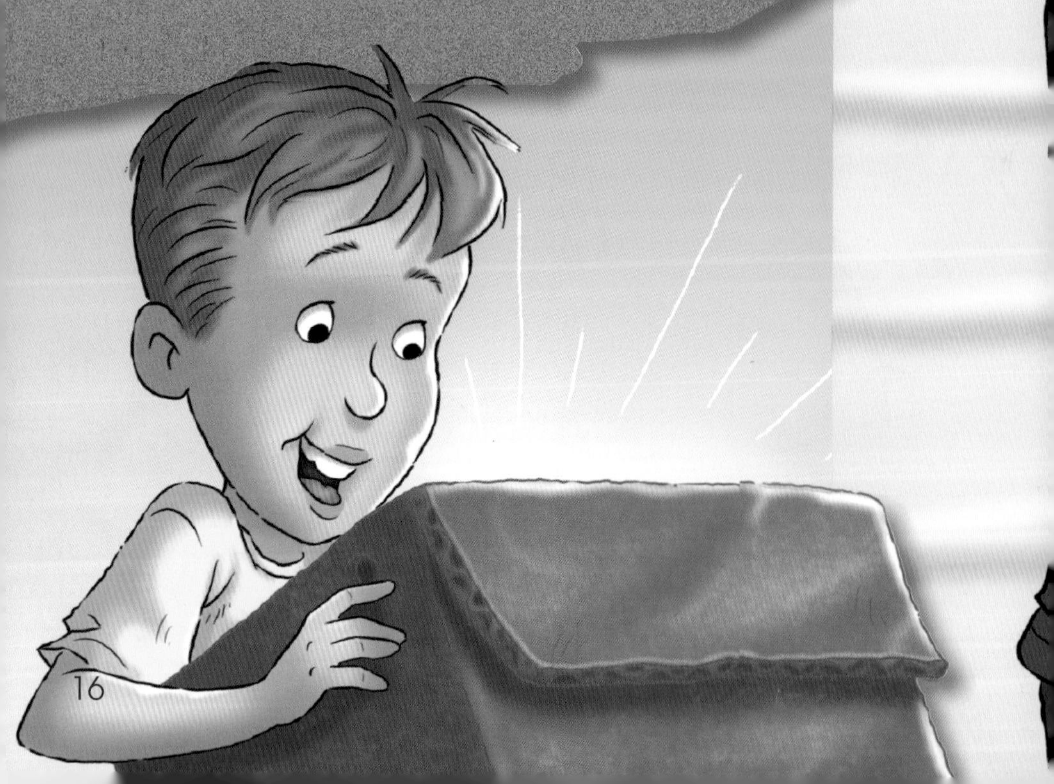

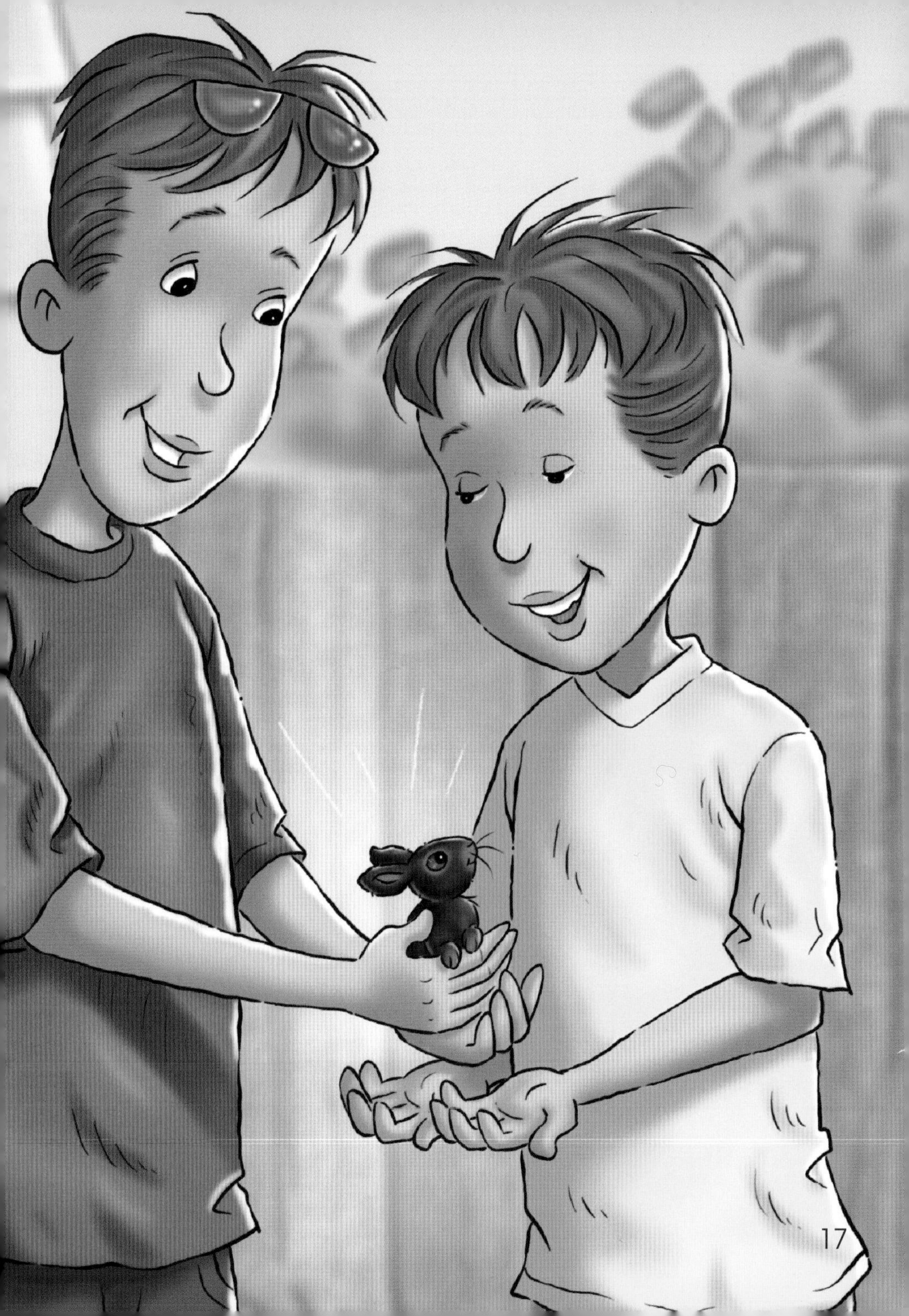

Recounts

Recounts tell about something that has happened.

A recount tells the reader:

- What happened

- To whom

- Where it happened

- When it happened

A recount tells events in sequence ...

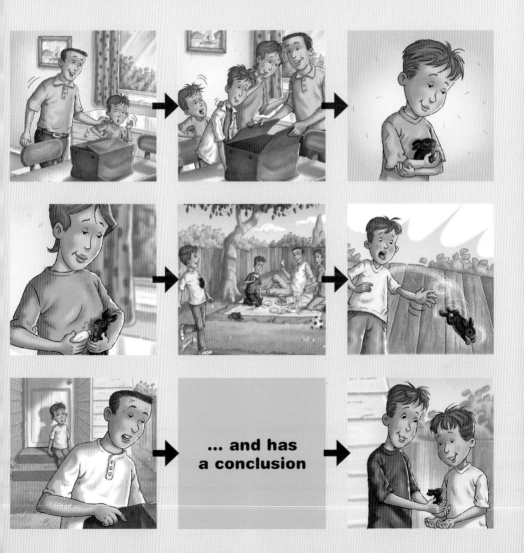

... and has a conclusion

Guide Notes

Title: The Black Rabbit
Stage: Fluency (2)

Text Form: Recount
Approach: Guided Reading
Processes: Thinking Critically, Exploring Language, Processing Information
Written and Visual Focus: Speech Bubbles

THINKING CRITICALLY
(sample questions)
- What do you think this story could be about? Look at the title and discuss.
- Look at the cover. What do you think the boys are talking about?
- Look at pages 2-3. What sort of person do you think Dad is? Why do you think that?
- Look at pages 4-5. How do you know that the narrator really wants to find out what is inside the box?
- Look at pages 6-7. Why do you think the baby rabbit was so scared?
- Look at pages 10-11. How do you know that the narrator is proud of Midnight?
- Look at pages 12-13. How do you think the narrator is feeling? Why do you think this?
- Look at pages 14-15. Why do you think the narrator said "I don't want to!" when his dad asked him to take one last look inside the box?

EXPLORING LANGUAGE

Terminology
Title, cover, illustrations, author, illustrator

Vocabulary
Clarify: pasture, huddled, pride, favorite
Nouns: bedroom, table, box, chest, sidewalk, furnace
Verbs: lay, picked, bury, knocked, drank, whispered
Singular/plural: flap/flaps, hand/hands
Simile: He was like a soft rag doll

Print Conventions
Apostrophes – contractions (won't, wasn't, it's)